The Visited

Krystle Havenar

BookLeaf Publishing

India | USA | LK

Presentation by *BookLeaf Publishing*

Web: www.bookleafpub.com

E-mail: info@bookleafpub.com

ISBN: 9789358317763

First edition 2023

*To mom and Caylee, I wish you could read this
with me. I love you*

Guests are coming

I awake
with thunder rumbling
in my heart
and lightning striking
my brain—
everyone
will be here tonight
and I
haven't prepared.

My sink
is full of dishes;
no time to dazzle them
with fine China,
I barely have time
to empty the debris
from the last visit—
The floors
stained with tar
and tears;
the walls
a mess
of honeyed handprints;
the rugs
covered
in mud.

And I can't
forget myself—
My hair,
left in tangles,
and my clothes
still on the bedroom floor
unwashed;
I am not suitable
for tonight's event.

They'll be here
any minute now,
I have to get up—
clean,
scrub,
paste a smile on my face
like nothing
is wrong.

Hurry now—
it won't be long.

Anxiety

You gently
crack the door,
quietly close it
behind you,
entering so peacefully
I didn't hear you coming.

You sneak around,
looking for me
and I know
you'll find me.
You may find me
peaceful,
scared,
busy,
exhausted,
happy-
All that you care
is that you
find me.

And once you've found me
you embrace me,
completely
envelope me

so that all I can hear
is your whispered
sweet nothings—

Nothing
I do
is good enough.
Nothing
I say
can ever be enough.
Nothing
will ever make me
enough
and nothing
can be done
to change it
because I
am nothing.

And you
overstay your welcome
so that I
can never quite tell
if you
are just coming
or just going.

Kudzu

You are not from here—
you were brought here
as a novelty,
an ornamental piece
of garden décor
and now you are called
the plant of the south.

They did not
understand you,
did not understand
the way you creep
and crawl,
that you grow
about a foot a day.
They couldn't guess
how fast your exploring leaves
would find new ground.
And they did not know
that your vines
root down every few feet,
that you
can put down roots
over
and over again,

making it so that
you now
exist everywhere
and nowhere
all at once.

You are a force
to be reckoned—
roots pulled up
and put back down.
They call you
the most infamous
weed.
And no one seems to remember
that you
didn't ask to be here,
you just learned
to survive
and thrive.

Rain

People have always tried
to predict your visits,
have been known
to dance,
pray,
and count lying cows
before they developed
a science of weather,
a way to estimate your likelihood
each day.

You visit
differently;
sometimes
you just barely
wave to us,
a few sprinkles
teasing the earth
as they fall
at our feet.

Other times,
you are steady,
working all day long
to nourish the soil

for our plants
and our souls.

Some days people curse you
for the others
you bring along
to prevent us
from working—
headaches and migraines
to make us rest;
wind,
thunder,
and lightning
to tend
to the needs of creation.

Yet you are always
a sustainer
of life—
dancing alongside us,
answering our prayers,
and assisting the world
in creating life
for all.

Tornado

Many of us live in your favorite haunts, places
you'd be remiss
if you didn't visit with regularity even though
we dread
your visits. You are so infamous that people
have
dedicated their lives to understanding you,
patterning your visits as if they
could be predicted.

You have lost some of your intrigue; we know
that you
are a culmination of opposites attracting, warm
updrafts meeting cool downdrafts
and having a whirlwind love affair,
so self-involved you pay
no mind to anything
in your path.
We can identify you
before you hit the ground,
rotations in the sky
slowly stretching downward,
trying to kiss
the earth
as you gain momentum.

And then we seek shelter from you, in
basements
and bathtubs, watching the news to hear
the people you have made local celebrities
tell us where you are,
where you have been,
and if
you seem to be leaving.

As your love fades, the sky celebrates,
painting itself an eerie greenish blue
and we can emerge
to take stock
of the property and lives lost
in your wake.

Butterflies

You emerge from your cocoons
en masse,
stretching your vibrant wings
in a coordinated dance
as your antennae
probe,
learning
the lay of the land
because all your eyes can see
is darkness,
wings,
and butterfly bodies.

I can feel each set of wings
beating in rhythm
to a song
only you know,
a frantic flying lesson
in my stomach.
Your antennae tickle a trail
along my stomach wall,
make me feel giddy;
and when you all get your wings
beneath you,
manage to fly

I feel as if my stomach
might fly
right out of my body.

You all serve me
as the sweetest signal
of something yet to come,
teach me
to savor each emergence
from your chrysalises
because these rare visits
are what life
is made of.

Author

He assembles words
the same way
a stonemason lays bricks
into complex creations;
buildings
that couldn't exist
if one brick—
one word
was different.

He weighs each word,
determines its value,
its context,
so that it can be fit
into the final product
like a puzzle piece.

He knows
how to manipulate words—
That words
are just strings of sound
he can use to convey meaning,
to express the beauty
of his creation—
he knows

how to put together words
to elicit
emotion.

And so when he said
he loved me
he already knew
there was no place for me
in his final draft.

Ruby-throated Hummingbird

I saw
a flicker of color
that made me think
of Christmas
in May,
heard the gentle whooshing
of wings
and thought
that to see you
I could leave offerings
all summer long—
One part sugar
to four parts water
left hanging
at all hours.

At first
you were hesitant;
visiting sparingly,
assessing the safety,
watching me
as I watched you,
watching me
faithfully refilling
your chalice
each week.

And one day
you amazed me
with the vibrancy
of your ruby-red throat
and the way your metallic green feathers
seemed to reflect the sunlight
back into the world around you,
creating space
for the magic
you hold.

My offerings never dwindled,
and with time
you allowed me
into your world
to marvel at your majesty
and beauty.
You rewarded me
graciously,
bringing your friends
and family
to dance around my shoulders
and sing sweet songs
just for me.
But your visits aren't meant
to be permanent—
I just hope
that next summer

my offerings
will still be accepted
by you.

Alyssa

She visited my life
at a time
that was pivotal—
I was young enough
to be naïve
and old enough
to start learning life,
to need guidance
to find my way.
My biography was full
of empty pages
stretching before us,
not knowing then
that each word written
during those years
would shape me
forever.

She wrote with gentleness,
with care,
co-authoring my high school years
and helping me find sure footing
in my future.

She hid proverbs
of spontaneity
between the lines
of how to make
the perfect brownies.
She left parables
of sisterhood,
of being able to choose
our own families;
how to pick each person
to know our secrets
would be kept safe
and that we wouldn't have to carry
each heavy weight.

And though she may not be
my co-author today,
I still find peace
in the wisdom she left me,
the lessons she hid
for when I was ready,
like how to fake a smile,
how to hide the hurt,
and,
how to know when I am ready
to share my voice
with the world.

Stars

Each night,
as the sun lays down to rest,
darkness could
overtake the sky
if it weren't
for you.

Your constellations
are my constant companions,
gracing each night sky,
never waxing
nor waning.

You are older
and more numerous
than the animals
that walk this earth,
yet you
exist as a unified whole,
lighting the path
of the past, present, and future.
You make our stories dance,
diamond-studded tales in the sky
of times past,
and times to come,

all while you
are memorizing us
and the stories
of our present.

People gaze at you
in awe,
name you individually—
Sirius, Castor, Vega, some still
unnamed—
name your clusters,
things like Orion's Belt,
Cassiopeia, Ursa Major
and Ursa Minor
just so that they can know
and honor
you,
our faithful
nightly visitors.

Brown tarantula

There were times
when I prepared for you in vain,
having only seen
your eight furry legs,
bulbous brown body,
and fur-encased fangs
in pictures.
I planned
escapes from you,
the fear-invoking spiders
I just knew
would be the death of me.
And when I lived
in the city,
you never came,
never quite seemed
real.

But now
I live in the country—
a rural hellscape
in late August
when all the males
emerge from their burrows,
following the pheromones

of females,
seeking to reproduce
and populating my roads
and my yard
with dozens
of these real-life terrors.

But now that I see you
quickly crossing roads,
hiding
when someone is near,
and scurrying away
from a barking dog,
I know that you,
while still a horrible sight,
are just a docile creature
playing your part
in the cycle of life,
just
like me.

The girl next door

Your laughter
comes to me in dreams,
a broken record
stuck on repeat,
constantly tittering
as I sort
through the memories—

Memories
of us as kids
playing in the garden,
only concerned
about the flowers,
carefully planned and tended to,
that blossomed
alongside us.
The days
spent at your kitchen table
comparing notes
on what the world
had taught us;
learning love,
learning hardships,
learning
how to survive.

The soundtrack fades
with the memory
of your parents' divorce
when you moved away,
leaving the house next door
empty
but for the echoes
of your giggles.

I've missed you
since then,
always longed
to hear that music
again
but now
the only chance I have
to hear your laugh
and see the sparkle
of your soul
is
within these dreams.

Death

You have the ability
to hide
around every corner,
to stealthily attack
whomever you please,
and you also have the patience
to stalk,
harass,
and torment your targets
should you choose.

You let some
see you ahead of time,
catch glimpses
of your black cloak
from the corner of their eye.
They have time
to adequately prepare for you,
to humbly receive you
as their guest,
leave the door unlocked
for you to quietly
steal them away.

Yet other times
you visit suddenly,
with no regard
to who you are choosing
or how
you will take them.
You only care
that you take someone.

You
are the most unpredictable visitor
I have ever known.
It is no wonder
people fear you.

Grief

You come to visit me
like an old friend,
waltzing through the front door,
wiping your muddy boots
on the pristine floors
I've spent years
scrubbing
as if you
were invited.

You come
bearing gifts;
tales of love,
the sound of laughter—
and you've wrapped each one
with the gut-wrenching image
of goodbye.

And I've tried
to lock the doors,
to mark your gifts
return to sender,
to wipe away
your black tar fingerprints
and each time

I think I've done it—
You
come
back.

Maybe one day
you'll bring new gifts,
flowers
of resilience
or honey-sweet tastes of life
that have been wrapped
with peaceful memories,
tied up with appreciation
and awe
for this world
and the people
I get to love.
But until that day comes,
I'll keep locking the doors
and scouring floors,
trying to right the mess you've made
of my mind.

The visitor

Walk with care
through this world—

Gingerly
take each step,
always observing
the world around
and below you
so that you can know the lives
each footfall
will affect.

Measure each word
you speak in this life—

Purposefully
compose your sentences,
always weighing the intent
against the scales of justice
so that we can breathe
love, kindness,
peace, and respect
into the lives
that hear us.

Knock gently
on each door
you intend to enter—

Because as often
as we are visited,
we are twice over
the visitor,
destroying
or enriching
someone else.

Out of tune piano

You have stood
for centuries,
a testament to craftsmanship,
and have adorned
all manner
of locales,
but sit regally now
in a pawn shop—
a picture
of grandiosity
and neglect.

You once
performed magnificently;
expert fingers
striking your keys
and gentle feet
pedaling in rhythm
to create masterpieces.
And you've also had
your keys mashed by children,
clumsy attempts
at learning your magic
that left your keys
oil-stained

and your seat
scratched.

You've moved
from place to place,
searching for a home
that will stand as long as you,
preferably temperature controlled
to avoid swelling
in the humidity.
You've dedicated yourself
to searching for careful hands
that will cherish you;
restore, tune, and honor
you
so that you can create beauty
once more.

Lottie, LA

You're a drive-by town,
positioned along a highway
so that anyone
who may want to visit
can only see
the houses with sagging roofs
and peeling paint
that resemble
a kindergarten art project
where they used too much glue.

Passersby see
a town on the edge
of falling apart,
a community only kept alive
by the people in it
because for miles,
all anyone can see
are ramshackle houses
and swamp.

Ancestral Homelands

"It is sacred",
they say of me
each time they care to visit,
"it holds the memories
and the history
of our people",
and I do.

I hold tales of resilience
in the tree roots
beneath their feet,
hold the memories
of families
torn apart
and ripped away from me
in the sulfur infused water
they have all
learned to purify.

But I do not feel sacred
much these days
with oil drills
stabbed into my bowels,
depleting the resources
I have spent centuries

guarding.
I do not feel sacred
when my people have left
and the scars of their ancestors
prevent their return
so that I
am left inhabited
by strangers
and spirits.

In times of celebration
when my people,
the people whose stories I've held
as long as they have called me
home,
return to me for a time,
then
I feel sacred.
But as I watch them leave
I feel the pain
of when they were ripped from me
anew;
my hardened, cracked surface
bearing the weight
of my loneliness
once more.

The Lake Aisles

Through the glass door
and to the right
sits a row of registers,
cashiers
scanning items,
checking IDs
and watching the clock
for their shift
to end.

The aisles
are evenly spaced,
laid out in the open
for all to see
as they enter.
Adults
sparsely dot the aisles
that are largely overrun
by students
from the next county over.

The students
are debating—
comparing costs,
deciding on quantities,

taking their time
wearily wading the aisles
in search
of their preferred Moscato.
They splash
towards sangrias,
rove
around the vodkas,
and lounge
in the rum;
they seek solace,
seek fun,
in a store
that has none.

Page Woodson School

You sprawl across the earth,
a bulky
crumbling red-brick juxtaposition
to the skyscrapers
and businesses
that have encroached
in your once lively
but since abandoned
domain.

Silence
roars around you,
but you hold
within your walls
the echoes
of laughter,
and of the footsteps
that once thundered
through your halls.

You were once
cherished,
receiving daily visits
from students
and teachers alike

and now
you are desolate—
you invoke fear
to all
who pass you by.

But there have been whispers
of your beauty,
thoughts
of renovation,
of making you,
a historic school,
into housing,
so maybe one day
you'll be visited
again.

Library book

I have no true home;
the closest thing
I have is a room,
lined with shelves
and myself,
sandwiched between others
waiting
to be wanted again;
to ride in cars,
sit on office desks,
be clumsily shoved
into backpacks
or rested gently
in a new bed.

I contain a story—
just one—
but a story
that people want
to read and experience
time and time again.

My pages
have known bookmarks,
receipts,

gum wrappers, photos, and napkins,
have had corners harshly folded
and unfolded
as a way
to hold the readers place.

I have been dropped in boxes,
left in the dark
until librarians can retrieve me,
place me lovingly
back on my shelf.
Some readers
have carried me gently,
warmly handed me back
to my keepers.
No matter how,
I always
find my way back.

I have heard more stories
than my pages
could ever hope to tell;
I learn something new
from each reader.
They may tear
my pages,
smear my carefully printed words,
or share their favorite drink
with me,

and even though
my words never change
I become something different,
something better
each time.

www.ingramcontent.com/pod-product-compliance
Lightning Source LLC
Chambersburg PA
CBHW061727130726
47996CB00006B/2532